# Paper

Helen Bliss

A & C Black · London

Designed by
**Jane Warring**

Illustrated by
**Lindy Norton**

Photography by
**Steve Shott**

Children's work by
George Abraham, Sarah Berjerano, Daniel Bergsagel,
Ilana Bergsagel, Camilla Bliss-Williams, Raffy Bliss-Williams,
Caroline Bresges, Florrie Campbell, Livonia Demetriou, Joshua Hay,
Daniel Hilton, Matthew McDougal, Miranda Segal, Amy Williams

First published in 1998 by
**A and C Black**
35 Bedford Row, London WC1R 4JH

Created by
**Thumbprint Books**

Copyright © 1998 Thumbprint Books

A CIP catalogue record for this book is available from the British Library

ISBN: 0 7136 4804 X (hbk)
ISBN: 0 7136 4805 8 (pbk)

Printed in Hong Kong by Wing King Tong Co Ltd

*Cover picture*: This papercut shows two cockerels
sitting on a Tree of Life. Papercuts like this were
made to decorate Polish houses at Easter time.

# Contents

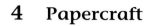
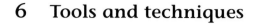

# Papercraft

Think how different the world would be if paper did not exist. There would be no books, comics or newspapers to read, no paper for writing letters, no banknotes or photographs.

Before paper was invented, people carved documents in stone or on tablets of clay. They also wrote on leaves, bark or animal skins. All of these things were much more difficult to write on than paper, and much bulkier to store.

Paper making was invented by a court official, named Ts'ai Lun, in China almost 2,000 years ago. The earliest paper was made from mulberry leaves, old rags and fish nets.

In Europe, until the end of the Middle Ages, books were written by hand on parchment, made from scraped and polished animal skins. It was only after the invention of printing in the 1450s that there was a big demand for paper. For a long time, paper was mostly made from old linen and cotton rags.

Today most paper is made from wood pulp. Millions of trees are grown just for paper making. Used paper can be recycled to make new paper.

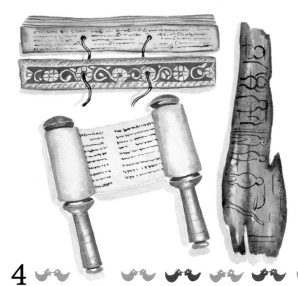

People have experimented with paper for hundreds of years. They have learned how to change its colour by printing and dyeing it. They have discovered how to mould or layer paper to make useful or decorative objects and they have hung cheerful paper decorations in their homes.

This book shows you six important paper techniques. It tells you how craftspeople all over the world use each technique to create very different sorts of objects.

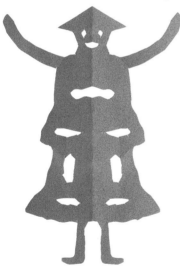

Try making your own papercuts and decorating paper with original designs. You can also learn how to make your own paper.

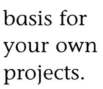

Discover how to shape paper into plates, funny ornaments or striking masks and puppets. Look at the objects made by children to help you. Once you have learned these techniques, use them as a basis for your own projects.

# Tools and techniques

The four main things you need for the projects in this book are paper, paints, scissors and glue.

## Paper

For papercuts, use thin paper, preferably coated with colour on one side only. For very delicate papercuts, use tissue paper. For the **stretched paper** projects use thin paper – layout paper is ideal. Recycle office waste or newspaper for **pulping**. Use blank waste paper for making **handmade paper**, because the inks in printed papers will make your paper grey. Newspapers and comics are excellent for **layering**.

## Scissors

Household scissors can be used for most projects, but small, straight nail scissors or small pointed craft scissors are essential for making detailed papercuts and for cutting through layered paper. Try pinking shears, or other scissors with zig-zag or wavy blades, for unusual effects.

## Simple snip technique

To make holes on the inside of your papercuts, gently pinch the paper between your thumb and forefinger and snip it. This makes a hole which you can then enlarge.

## Paper pulp recipe

Fill a third of a bucket with paper torn into 2 cm pieces. Ask an adult to pour hot water on top. Leave it to soak and cool for 20 minutes. Then stir it hard with a wooden spoon until the paper begins to break up.

Put a handful of this mixture into a liquidiser or food processor and cover it well with water. Ask an adult to liquidise this in short bursts (so as not to strain the motor) until the pulp is smooth. Repeat with more handfuls of pulp until it is all liquidised. This pulp is ready now to use for papermaking. It can be kept in a fridge in a sealed container.

## Moulding pulp

Drain as much liquid as you can from wet pulp, using a sieve. Add a cup of PVA glue to each bucket of pulp that you have made. Clean plastic margarine tubs, plastic and foil food packaging can all be used as moulds, as well as china plates and bowls. Cover them with cling film. When you cover a mould with pulp, make sure the pulp is at least 1 cm thick.

## How to layer a paper mask

Balance a blown-up balloon in a bowl to keep it upright. Tear newspaper and old comics into 2 cm pieces. Keep the two kinds of paper separate.

Mix equal amounts of PVA glue and water in a bowl. Dip newspaper pieces, one by one, into the mixture and brush them on to the balloon.

When the balloon is half-covered, glue on a layer of comic pieces. Glue on alternate layers of newspaper and comic pieces, until you have at least six layers. If these become too wet, put on a layer of dry newspaper.

## Making eye holes in a layered mask

Put the mask up to your face. Ask a friend to draw circles on it, in roughly the position where your eyes are. Ask an adult to cut out these eye holes with sharp scissors, as the paper layers are very stiff.

## Getting ready for marbling and paper making

Marbling and paper making are very wet activities. Cover the table with plenty of newspaper to soak up water. If you're very messy, cover the floor with newspaper as well. Wear an old shirt or apron and wear a pair of thin plastic gloves.

After marbling, ask an adult to help you clean your equipment with a soft cloth soaked in white spirit. Wash your hands thoroughly with soap and water.

# Pretty papercuts

Papercuts have been made for over 1,000 years. They often show details of the life and beliefs of the people who make them. They are still used for decorations at festivals, birthdays, weddings and even funerals.

Cai Xiaoli

A Chinese artist made a papercut of this tiger-cat to pin on the bed of a newborn child. It has a special meaning. The Chinese believe that it will both protect and amuse the child. The colour red means joy.

The Chinese also make papercuts to decorate windows and lanterns as well as for sticking on walls. Papercutting skills are handed down from one generation to another, often from mother to daughter.

In Mexico, a riot of bright colours is used for these delicate papercut banners. They are strung across streets and yards at religious festivals, such as Christmas and the Day of the Dead.

Skilled Mexican artists put fifty sheets of thin tissue paper in a stack. They punch a design through all of them at once, using a hammer and a thin, sharp chisel.

Every Easter in Poland, people used to spring clean and whitewash their cottages and make new papercuts to decorate their rooms. Every region had its own designs.

Polish people in Kurpie used sheep shears to cut a Tree of Life from a single sheet of paper. They also made cut-outs with layers of contrasting colours, like this bright bird.

In the Lowicz region of Poland, people created colourful rows of characters in folk - costumes, dancing, playing music and travelling by horse or bicycle. These were carefully made from separate pieces of paper stuck very precisely next to one another.

# Clever cut-outs

Try making your own papercuts from thin coloured paper or fine tissue, using small, sharp nail scissors. Experiment with pinking shears and scissors with wavy blades as well. Start with simple shapes and then progress to more fiddly ones.

### The Tree of Life

Fold a large sheet of paper in half. Draw one half of a tree on the top fold, with its trunk parallel with the crease. Make the branches swirly or straight and include smooth or spiky leaves, lush flowers and roosting birds. Shade the areas you need to cut out. Then carefully snip around the tree outline. Do not cut too near the fold. Open it out and see the result!

## Imaginary animals

Make a dragon-dog, a bird-fish or any other sort of fantasy animal. Draw your creature on coloured paper, decorating it with shapes and patterns. Cut it out. Cut out the inner lines using the 'snip' technique (see page 6).

Make some birds in the same way. Add layers of decoration, cut from squares of gummed paper in contrasting colours. Glue them on top of your cut-out or under the holes, so that they show through.

## Festive flags

Make several flags that you can string together to make a banner for your room or a party. Draw your design in chalk on some tissue paper and shade the bits you want to cut out. Make a border around the edges, which should be especially wide at the top.

Put the finished flags in a row. Lay a long piece of string across their top edges. Fold these edges over the string and glue them down.

# Decorated delights

The earliest decorated papers were used as prayer offerings at Japanese temples. In Europe for the last 400 years, decorated papers have mainly been used for book covers and endpapers.

These Milky Way swirls were made by dropping coloured inks on to a gel made of carragheen moss, and drawing patterns in it with a stick or brush. When a sheet of paper is laid on top, the inks stick to the paper. This effect is called marbling.

In ancient Japan, patterns were made by fanning and blowing the inks into fantastic shapes. In Turkey, fine needles were used to draw hyacinth and tulip shapes in the inks. In Europe, brushes and combs are still used to create incredible patterns.

*Solveig Stone, Compton Marbling*

Another way of marbling is to drop oil paint on top of water and swirl it into patterns. The oil does not mix with the water, so, when a sheet of paper is laid on top, the oil paint sticks to it.

These boxes are covered with paste paper. To make paper like this, a thick, coloured flour paste is brushed over a plain sheet of damp paper.

The patterns are made by dragging combs, sticks or fingers through the paste while it is still wet. This reveals the colour of the paper underneath.

Hill people in Nepal decorate paper by printing it with wood blocks which show everyday images. They use inks made from vegetable dyes. The paper is made by boiling up daphne tree bark into a pulpy mush. This is sieved to make flat sheets, which are then dried.

# Patterns and prints

Make your own decorated paper for covering books and boxes or wrapping presents for your family and friends. You can use almost any kind of paper, including tissue and brown parcel paper.

## Mysterious marbling

This is very messy, so cover a table with lots of newspaper before you start. Ask a grown-up to help you thin some oil paint in a jam jar, with enough white spirit to make it run like milk. Use a separate jar and brush for each colour.

Line a baking tray with tin foil. Almost fill it with cold water. Sprinkle several colours of paint on to the water with a brush. Swirl the paint gently with a stick to make patterns. Wearing rubber gloves, lower a sheet of paper on to the water. Making sure there are no air bubbles, lift the paper off the water, and put it, paint side up, on to a sheet of newspaper. Dab another sheet of paper on the surface of the water to clean it, before you try marbling again.

## Printed papers

Draw designs on to two or three thin kitchen sponges with a ball point or felt-tip pen. Carefully cut them out with small, sharp scissors. Cut pieces of corrugated card, slightly larger than the sponge shapes. Glue each shape to a piece of card with waterproof glue.

Dab water-based paint on to a sponge shape and press it on to a sheet of paper. Gently rub the back of the card. Lift it up and hey presto! Mix and match the shapes to print a pattern all over the paper.

## Dragged designs

Mix one tablespoon of cornflour with a cup of water in a pan. Ask an adult to stir it on a low heat, until it goes clear. Let it cool. Mix in some paint. Brush it on to a sheet of paper. Draw designs in it with a comb or your fingers.

15

# Handmade paper

Paper has been made by hand for over 2,000 years. In Nepal and Japan, handmade papers are still created using the same simple methods that papermakers have used for centuries.

Handmade paper is made from pulped rags or long plant threads, called fibres, that will tangle together to make a flat sheet. Banana leaves, straw, sugar cane and even waterweed can be used to make paper.

The paper shown above is only made once a year, in summer. The papermakers collect flowers from meadows around their papermill in France. They mix them into paper pulp, so that the flowers become part of the paper.

To make paper pulp, rags or plants are pounded and soaked in a vat of water. Two frames, called a mould and deckle, are scooped into the vat and lifted out again. Water drains through the fine wire mesh of the mould, leaving behind a thin layer of matted fibres, held in place by the deckle. This layer is pressed and dried into a sheet of paper.

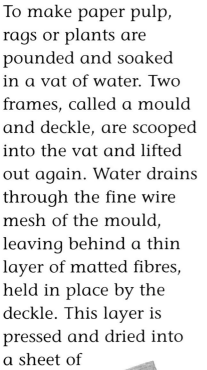

*mould*

*deckle*

These papers are handmade in south Indian villages. They are made from recycled cotton rags and are very strong. Artists use them for painting and printing.

The fine washi or Japanese paper below is made from the bark stripped from a type of mulberry tree. The lacy effect is made by dripping water through a stencil on to a freshly made sheet of paper. The pink paper is made by mixing cotton threads and shiny gold flecks into the pulp.

# Glorious colours

Make your own paper, using the recipe for paper pulp on page 6. Make any colour paper you like. Sprinkle it with seeds or flowers or make some striking paper pulp pictures. These stunning papers are great for making unusual and original greetings cards.

## Flowery fun

Spread some pulp on to a dish cloth. Lay pressed flowers and leaves all over it, either at random or in a pattern. Put another cloth on top. Press it with a rolling pin. Remove the top cloth and leave the pulp to dry into paper. Try using shiny sweet wrappers or string instead of flowers.

## Pasta and seeds

Mix acrylic or powder paint into a handful of paper pulp to colour it. Stir in some seeds, glittery sequins or dried pasta. Put a thick pad of newspaper on your work surface and lay a clean kitchen cloth on top of it.

Spread the pulp evenly over the cloth, shaping it into a rectangle. Lay a second cloth on top. Press it all over with your hands or a rolling pin. Peel off the top cloth and leave the pulp to dry and become a sheet of paper.

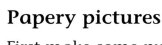

## Papery pictures

First make some pulp in several different colours, using coloured papers.

Spread a kitchen cloth on top of a thick wad of newspaper. Shape a picture on the cloth using the pulp. You can put one colour on top of another, as well as putting the colours side by side.

Put a second cloth on top of your picture and press it gently to squeeze out excess water. Take off the top cloth and put your picture in a warm place to dry.

# Painted pulp

Paper pulp is very cheap and easy to mould. For centuries, people all over the world have used it to make everyday objects such as bowls and boxes. It is so strong that it has also been used to make tables, chairs and even a warrior's helmet.

This decorated paper plate comes from Russia and is painted in the 'Khokhloma' style. Khokhloma was a fortress where, 400 years ago, peasants sold wooden bowls, spoons and furniture that they hand-painted with jewel-like colours.

Today, plates like this are moulded from paper pulp in Russian factories. Artists paint swirly leaves, bright flowers and juicy berries on them in red, black and gold. They paint these straight on to the plates without drawing first.

These model animals come from Bihar in north-east India, where paper pulp toys have been made for centuries by women for their children. About 30 years ago, after a big famine, villagers started making them to sell to tourists. This earned the villagers extra money to feed and support their families.

Paper pulp boxes like these were first made in Kashmir, northern India, with pulp left over from papermaking. Long ago, such boxes were made to hold camel-hair brushes used for miniature painting. Kashmiris now make paper pulp bowls and candlesticks, as well as boxes. These are finely painted with flowers and animals.

# Mashed magic

Become a magician and turn drab grey paper pulp into fabulous animals, plates and boxes for everyone to marvel at. See pages 6 and 7 for instructions on how to make and mould the pulp. Let the pulp dry completely between each stage.

## Bunny box

Make enough pulp to cover two small identical bowls and to shape a bunny. Wrap the outside of the bowls with cling film. Cover them with pulp. When they are dry, separate the pulp boxes from the bowls. Peel off the cling film. Trim the boxes so that they fit together.

Shape a bunny from the extra pulp. Press it on the wet box lid. Cut out card ears and push them into the rabbit's head. When the box and rabbit are dry, paint them both in glowing colours.

## Pulpy plates

Cover the underside of a rimmed plate with cling film. Roll a ball of pulp big enough to fit over it. Put the pulp on the centre of the plate and gently spread it evenly all over the bottom of the plate with your fingers. Leave the pulp to dry in a warm place for at least a day when it will have dried into a plate shape.

Carefully separate the pulp plate from the china plate and peel off the cling film. Trim the edges of the pulp plate and paint it in bold colours. Varnish your plate with PVA glue to make it shiny.

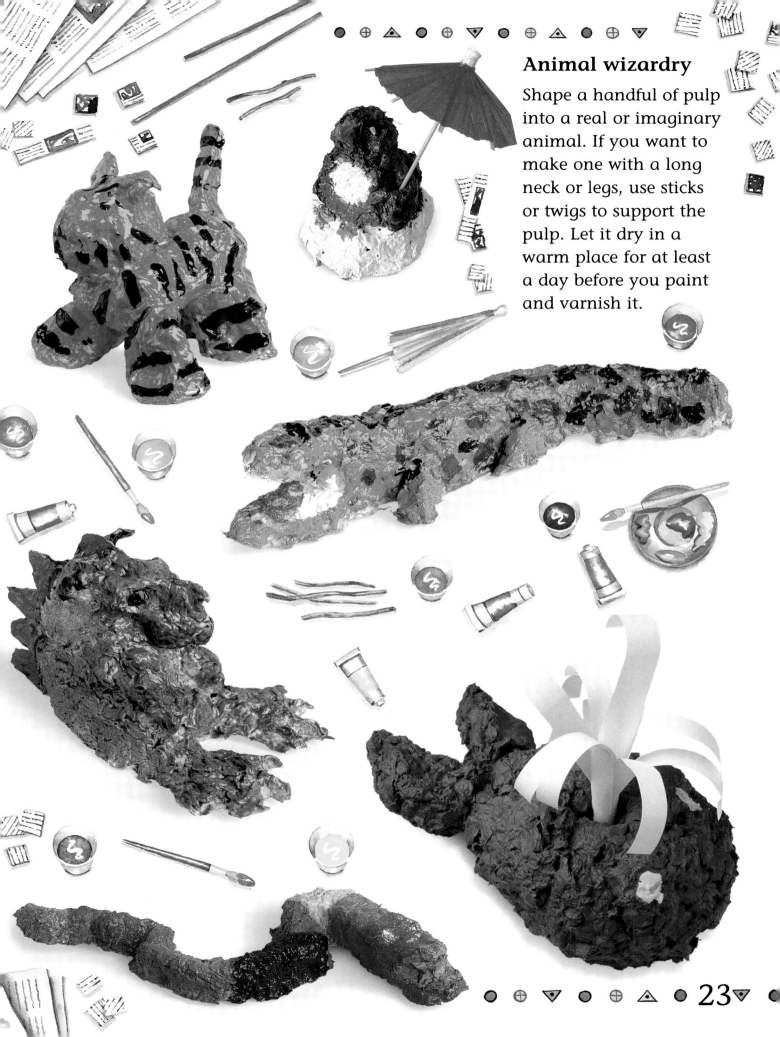

## Animal wizardry

Shape a handful of pulp into a real or imaginary animal. If you want to make one with a long neck or legs, use sticks or twigs to support the pulp. Let it dry in a warm place for at least a day before you paint and varnish it.

# Layered paper

Paper can be layered and glued over a shaped mould to produce an exact copy, perfect in every detail. Artists and craftspeople have used this cheap, strong material to make expressive faces for puppets, figures and masks.

This wicked wolf licking his lips and the friendly bear are glove puppets inspired by characters in European folk tales. They have hollow layered paper heads. Puppeteers can put their fingers inside to make them nod and shake.

A head is shaped first in modelling clay and paper is layered on top. Once the paper head has dried, it is cut in half and the clay mould is removed. The head is stuck together again with more paper layers before it is painted.

Japanese actors wear these small masks for comical plays they perform at festivals in country villages.

The masks represent gods, demons and cunning animals, such as a fox and a monkey, as well as humans. Each character has a particular expression which the audience can immediately recognise.

In the 1700s, travelling troupes of actors used to perform funny masked plays, called Commedia dell' Arte, in the town squares of Italy. The actors had fixed characters, but no script.

Each character wore a particular costume and half-mask, which gave clues about his or her age and personality. The masks covered only the eyes and nose, so that actors could show changes of mood with their mouths.

Every year, in November, Mexicans celebrate the Day of the Dead when they remember their dead relatives. They decorate their houses and offer food and flowers to the dead.

As part of these celebrations, artists make a joke about the scariness of death by creating humorous paper and wire skeletons. These are often dressed in bright clothes, doing everyday things, such as eating or riding a bicycle.

# Loads of layers

Layered paper is perfect for making masks for fancy-dress parties, puppet-heads and models to keep or give away as presents. All you need is a shape to mould the paper over – such as a blown-up balloon, scrumpled paper, soft wire or pipe-cleaners.

## Marvellous masks

Cover half a balloon with six layers of newspaper and glue mix (see page 7). If you want to make a special character, scrumple pieces of newspaper to shape its ears, eyebrows or nose. Glue them on to the top layer. Let the newspaper dry, then remove the balloon.

Mark two holes for your eyes and cut them out (see page 7). Paint and decorate your mask. Make a hole on either side and fit through a length of elastic long enough to fit around your head. Knot the ends together.

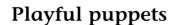

## Playful puppets

Scrunch up some newspaper into a ball. Push a short cardboard tube into it and tape the two together. Carefully glue six layers of torn paper over the 'head' and 'neck'. Glue on scrumpled paper ears, a nose and antennae.

Leave the puppet to dry, then paint its face. Cut two identical pieces of felt in the shape of a dress with long sleeves. Sew or glue the edges together, making sure that the neck of the dress is big enough to fit around the cardboard neck. Glue the dress to the neck. Give your puppet a collar of ribbon or felt and hands made out of felt or paper.

## Wiry wonders

Bend soft wire or pipe cleaners into the shape of a hollow animal, bird or person. Use masking tape to join the arms, legs and any other features firmly together.

Carefully pack the wire model with either scrumpled tissue paper or polyester stuffing. Loosely wind masking tape over it to hold the stuffing in place. Brush glue over the masking tape and lay several layers of tissue on top, until the surface is smooth. Use brightly coloured paint mixed with PVA glue to decorate your model.

# Festivals and fun

In China and Japan, people discovered that if they stretched paper over wooden or bamboo frames they could make strong but very lightweight structures. In the past, many Japanese houses even had stretched paper windows and walls.

Children in China, Hong Kong, London and San Francisco wear a lion head-dress like this, made from bamboo and paper, to celebrate Chinese New Year. On New Year's Day, people gather for a huge procession through the streets.

Dancing men carry a long paper lion with a gigantic head on sticks. They shake its head and twist its body to the beat of drums. As they pass shops and houses, they catch money and lettuce dangling from the doorways.

Every spring in China and Japan there are kite fighting festivals. People glue powdered glass on their own kite strings. This makes them razor sharp so they can cut through the strings of other competitors' kites. The kites, made of paper and bamboo, are painted with animals or famous ancient warriors. Some of them are so enormous that dozens of people are needed to help control them, but they can still fly because they are so light.

In Japan, before electric lights existed, people used paper lanterns with candles inside to light their homes.

Small box lanterns, which could fold up when not in use, were used for travelling.

This toro, or religious lantern, is made from paper and hangs outside a Buddhist temple. Toro lanterns were originally used to provide light for monks during their long night-time meditations or for lighting the altar.

Kites were invented over 2,000 years ago by the Chinese and used by their army. Strapped to huge kites, men were sent flying into the air to spy over enemy camps or to fire arrows at unsuspecting soldiers below. Kites have also been used in religious ceremonies and were seen as a link between heaven and earth.

# Stretched shapes

Use ordinary thin garden sticks with fine paper stretched over them to make your own kites, lamp and head-dresses. They are all very lightweight and can be made to whatever size you choose.

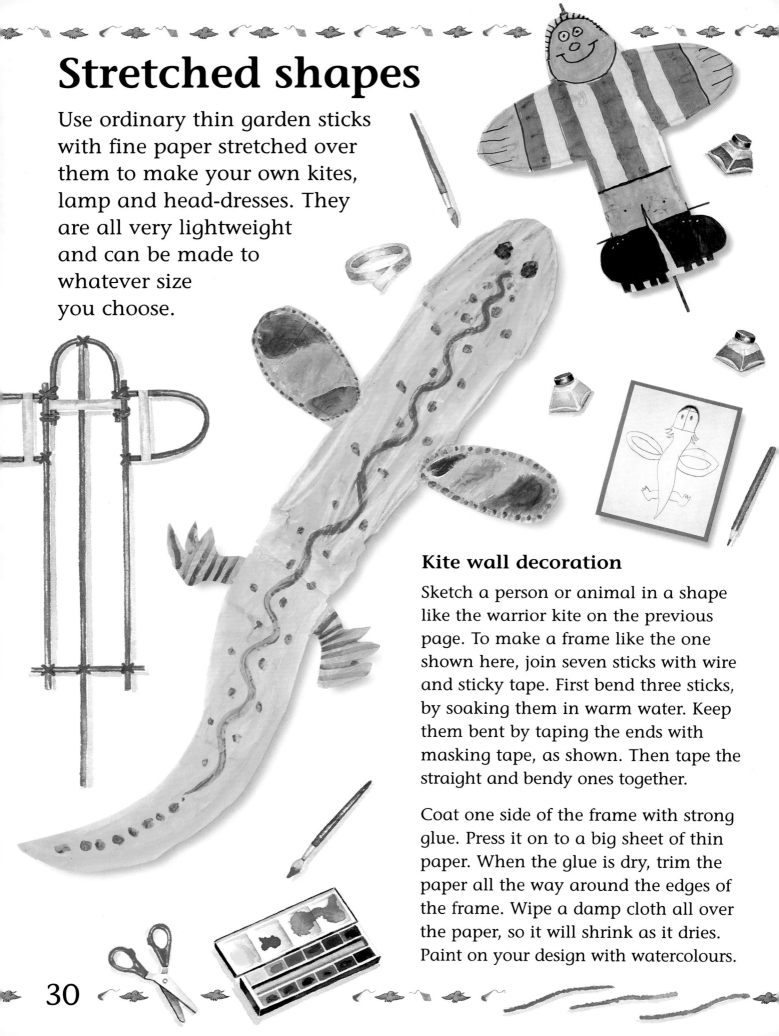

## Kite wall decoration

Sketch a person or animal in a shape like the warrior kite on the previous page. To make a frame like the one shown here, join seven sticks with wire and sticky tape. First bend three sticks, by soaking them in warm water. Keep them bent by taping the ends with masking tape, as shown. Then tape the straight and bendy ones together.

Coat one side of the frame with strong glue. Press it on to a big sheet of thin paper. When the glue is dry, trim the paper all the way around the edges of the frame. Wipe a damp cloth all over the paper, so it will shrink as it dries. Paint on your design with watercolours.

## Shadow lamp

Join eight sticks into a pyramid with wire and sticky or masking tape. Cut four triangles of thin paper, 1 cm larger all round than each side of the pyramid. Attach the triangles to the sides with strong glue.

When the glue has dried, trim off the edges of the paper. Cut out some tissue paper shapes, such as flowers, trees, stars or animals, to glue on to the inside of the lamp with a glue stick. Close the curtains, put a torch inside your lamps and enjoy the shadows!

## Monster head-dress

Use sticks to make a strong pyramid frame, large enough to fit your head inside. Add extra sticks to the pyramid both to strengthen it and to make a monster head shape that you really like.

Cover each section of the frame (apart from the opening for your head) with thin paper as before. Paint the head in bright watercolours. Add tassels, feathers, sweet wrappers, sequins and other decorations to make a truly striking, scary monster.

# Index

## Acknowledgements

*The author and publishers are grateful to the following shops, galleries and individuals for their help with this book:* Clifford Birt, R.K. Birt, paper importers; Kate Brett, marbler; Centaur Gallery; Chris Clayton, Paperchase; Sandra Evans Gibbs, paste paper; John Gillow; Minnie Kumria, Soma Books; Jane Townsend, King Alfred School; Mike Lock, Nepal Trading; Nigel MacFarlane, Khadi Papers; Ray Man Musical Instruments; Benjamin Pollock's Toy Shop; Solveig Stone, Compton Marbling; Cai Xiaoli and Jainin Wang.

*The publishers are also grateful to the following for permission to reproduce the illustrations on the pages mentioned.*
Page 8: Cai Xiaoli; page 13: Solveig Stone, Compton Marbling; page 28: Ray Man Musical instruments.

## Stockists

You can buy materials for the projects in this book from any large department store or art shop. If you prefer, you can buy them mail order from the following specialist suppliers:

**Specialist papers**
*Falkiner Fine Papers*, 76 Southampton Row, London WC1B 4AR
Telephone: 0171 831 1151  Fax: 0171 430 1248
*Paperchase*, 213 Tottenham Court  Road, London W1P 9AF
Telephone 0171 589 8496  Fax: 0171 637 1225

**Marbling materials**
*Compton Marbling*, Lower Lawn Barns, Tisbury, Wiltshire SP3 6SG
Telephone: 01747 871147  Fax: 01747 871265
*T. N. Lawrence and Son Ltd*, 119 Clerkenwell Road, London EC1R 5BY
Telephone: 0171 242 3534

**Teachers' resources and information for Indian crafts**
*Soma Books*, 38 Kennington Lane, London SE11 4LS
Telephone: 0171 735 2101  Fax: 0171 735 3076

**Children's wavy-edged craft scissors and pinking shears**
*Early Learning Centre*, South Marston Park, Swindon SN3 4TJ
Telephone: 0990 352 352